Blue

Blue is mentioned in the Bible
Fifty times or more
Because this color once adorned
The robes that rich kings wore.
There are many things, of course,
That God has colored blue,
Like robins' eggs, sweet blueberries,
The sky and oceans too.
Spring flowers such as bluebells that
Will grow most anywhere
Are also blue like bluebirds and
The blue jeans that we wear.
When God created all the colors
I am so glad that He thought up
The pretty color—blue.

Colorful Clues

Solve these riddles. Then write the answers in the boxes of the crossword puzzle on page 3.

ACROSS

3. I'm famous as a songbird, and
   God made me brilliant red.
   My feathers form a pointed crest
   On top my pretty head.

   _____

4. When I fan my feathers, it's
   A sight you won't forget.
   No wonder King Solomon
   Made me his royal pet.

   _____

5. Many birds know how to sing,
   But few know how to talk.
   I don't know what I'm saying, but
   Your words I'll wisely mock.

   _____

DOWN

1. God gave me quite a lovely voice.
   "Cheer-up, cheer-cheer!" I sing,
   For I'm that bird with a red breast
   Who greets you every spring.

   _____

2. When first you see me in the spring,
   I'm sure you will rejoice.
   I have the bluest feathers, and
   A happy singing voice.

   _____

3. Inside my cage I'll swing and sing,
   Tweet-tweeting all day long.
   My colors are quite beautiful,
   And so is my sweet song.

   _____

Solve the Crossword

Write your answers from page 2 in the boxes to finish the crossword puzzle.

A Bell That Doesn't Ring

Can you solve this riddle? The answer is the name of a bell that doesn't ring.

My blossoms grow along a stem
That sways when breezes sigh.
My color matches perfectly
The color of God's sky.
Although there's *bell* within my name,
You'd never hear me ring,
For I'm a dainty flower that
Starts blooming in the spring.
People say I'm pretty when
They catch a glimpse of me.
Two easy words make up my name…
They both begin with *B*.

b _ _ _   b _ _ _

Many Kinds of Bells

There are many kinds of bells. People used bells even in Bible times. When Aaron became the first high priest of Israel, he wore bells around the hem of his robe so that people could hear him entering the temple. Today we like to hear church bells ring, calling us to praise God.

All of the bells on this page—except for one—were made by people. Circle the one bell that God made. Then color it blue.

How Many Eggs?

Color the robin's nest. Color the eggs blue. Count the eggs. How many eggs are in the nest?

Thank You, God, for Pockets

What things on this page could you put in your blue jeans' pocket? Draw a line from each object to a pocket.

7

God's Good Creation

After God created the blue oceans, He made many different fish. How many can you count?

Yellow

Bright buttercups and dandelions—
These things are sunny yellow.
Bananas, corn, and butter too,
And jiggly, lemon Jell-O.
God made this *happy* color, and
I'm sure that everyone
Smiles when they see yellow 'cause
It's like the summer sun.

Find the objects that are yellow and color them this happy color.

Praise God for His Gift of Food

The food God gives us comes in many different colors. Say a thank-You prayer to God for the good food He gives you. Then match the numbers to color the food. Circle the foods that are yellow.

1. yellow   2. green   3. blue   4. red

A Colorful Weed in God's World

I am a yellow lion who
Tries very hard to growl
At all the people walking by
Who look at me and scowl.
I wish that I could bravely roar
And ruffle up my fur,
But I'm a *dandelion* and
I cannot even purr.

Some dandelions have started to grow in some nice, green grass. *Pull up* the dandelions by crossing them out with a yellow crayon.

Praise God for Bananas

Slice it on your cereal,
Or pack it in a lunch.
"Yummy-yum" you'll surely say,
If Mom brings home a bunch.

Find the bananas in the fruit basket and color them yellow.

Thank You, God, for Corn

Try nibbling me from off the cob.
Each kernel is yum-yummy.
And when I'm popped, I'll make a treat
To fill your hungry tummy.

Draw a line through the maze and help the bunny find his way out of the corn field.

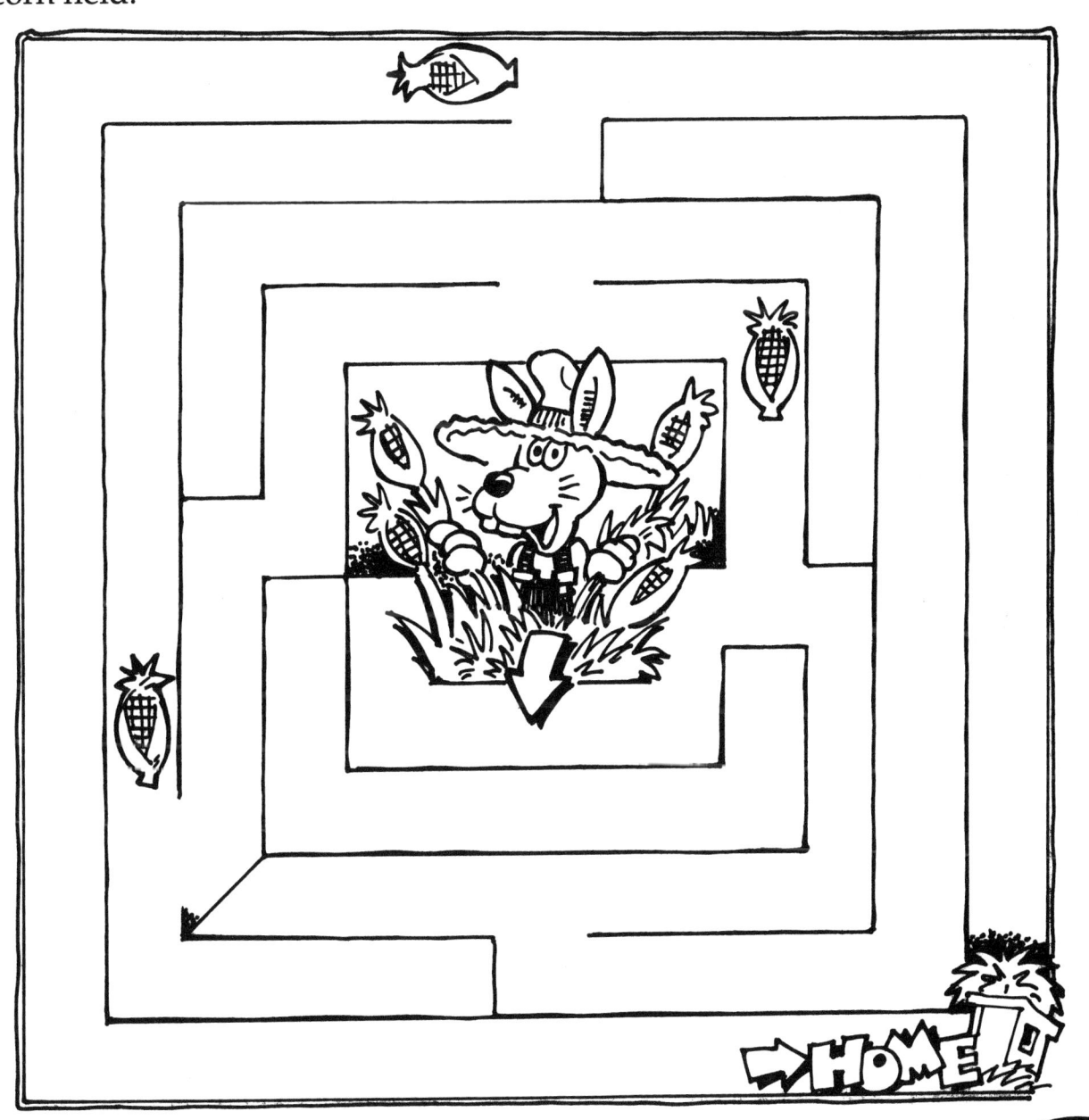

Butter Is Yellow

People in Bible times made butter from the milk of sheep, goats, and camels. People probably first made butter by shaking milk in a bag made of animal skin.

On which of these things would you spread butter? Circle them with a yellow crayon.

Solve the Riddle

When breezes blow 'cross grassy fields,
You'll see me sway and flutter.
Then hold me underneath your chin
To see if you like butter.
The last word in my name is *cup*,
But you can't drink from me,
For I'm a yellow flower that
Begins with letter *B*.

Color these flowers yellow.

b _ _ _ _ _ _ c u p

God's Yellow Gifts

God gives us many gifts with the happy color yellow. Find and circle the following words hidden in this box.

SUN   DANDELION   CORN   YELLOW   BUTTER   BANANA   LEMON

S	U	N	A	D	A	N	D	E	L	I	O	N
R	Q	P	O	N	M	L	K	J	I	H	G	F
T	S	C	B	D	C	Y	Z	X	A	K	U	V
Q	W	O	E	R	T	E	Y	U	I	O	P	A
S	D	R	F	G	H	L	B	U	T	T	E	R
J	K	N	L	Z	X	L	C	V	B	N	M	G
R	T	Y	U	I	O	O	B	A	N	A	N	A
L	E	M	O	N	P	W	Q	W	E	R	T	Y

Green

Mom gives us good advice when she
Tells us to eat our greens,
Like spinach, sprouts, and broccoli,
Peas, lettuce, and green beans.
Whenever we see food that's green,
We know it's good for us.
Can you think of another one?
Of course! Asparagus!
God made so many things in shades
Of green for you and me.
We only have to look around
And maybe we will see
Pickles, grass, and pretty trees,
And leaves of every kind.
Now, green is everywhere we look.
It's not so hard to find.

An Indoor Garden

Now, when the sun is hiding, and
Cold snow is in the air,
Wouldn't it be nice to see
Green growing plants somewhere?
Your windowsill would be just fine—
Or dresser, if you wish—
A fish tank or a jar will do,
And sometimes just a dish.
Now, follow these instructions, and
Then anytime can be
Just like summer in your room…
A warming sight to see.

God Gives Us Green Plants

Make a Water Garden

Vegetables make pretty water gardens. Carrots, sweet potatoes, and horseradishes grow well in water.

Lay a large sweet potato in a shallow dish and pour in enough water to half-cover it. Ask an adult to help you cut a few inches off the tops of carrots and horseradishes and set the tops in shallow dishes of water.

Place your garden in or near a window. Check the water in each dish twice a week and add more when necessary.

Make a Hothouse Garden

A small fish tank or glass jar can make a hothouse garden. Ask an adult to help you find a glass top for the container. Place a layer of charcoal in the bottom of the tank or jar. Then add a layer of pebbles, then a layer of soil.

Dig up some small plants to put in your garden. Be sure to leave a little ball of soil around the roots. Ferns, mosses, and lichens grow well in a hothouse garden. Or you may buy some tiny plants.

Arrange the plants in the soil and sprinkle with water. Place a small piece of cardboard on the rim of the tank to allow a small airway between the glass top and the tank.

Set your hothouse garden near a sunny window. Sprinkle the garden each week. The water will rise up from the plants and stick to the glass top. It will then fall on the plants like raindrops. That is God's plan for watering the beautiful plants He created.

I Like Green

Use a green crayon to draw a line from the word *green* to each green object.

A Miracle in God's Wonderful World

Have you ever wondered how a tiny seed grows into a beautiful plant or tree? It is truly a miracle in God's wonderful world! Follow the instructions on this page to watch a seed grow.

Soak seeds (peas, lima beans, corn, radish) in water overnight. Wet a piece of blotter paper and use it to line the inside of a clear glass. Poke the seeds between the sides of the glass and the blotter paper. Pour a small amount of water into the bottom of the glass each day to keep the blotter wet. Watch roots, stems, and little leaves grow from the seeds.

A Nature Scrapbook

God created many kinds of leaves. It's fun to collect leaves and put them in a scrapbook or photo album. You may want to collect green leaves in the spring and summer, and gather the same kinds of leaves in autumn when they have changed colors.

Find leaves with stems attached. Place each leaf on a pad of newspaper, then cover the leaf with a piece of wax paper. Ask an adult to help you press the wax paper with a hot iron. Glue or tape leaves in a scrapbook. Cover each page with a sheet of cellophane.

To make a scrapbook of wildflowers, place each flower between two sheets of newspaper before closing it in the middle of a big book. The newspaper will absorb moisture from the flower so it won't become moldy. Change the newspaper several times until the flower is flat and dry. Then tape the flower in your scrapbook and cover it with cellophane.

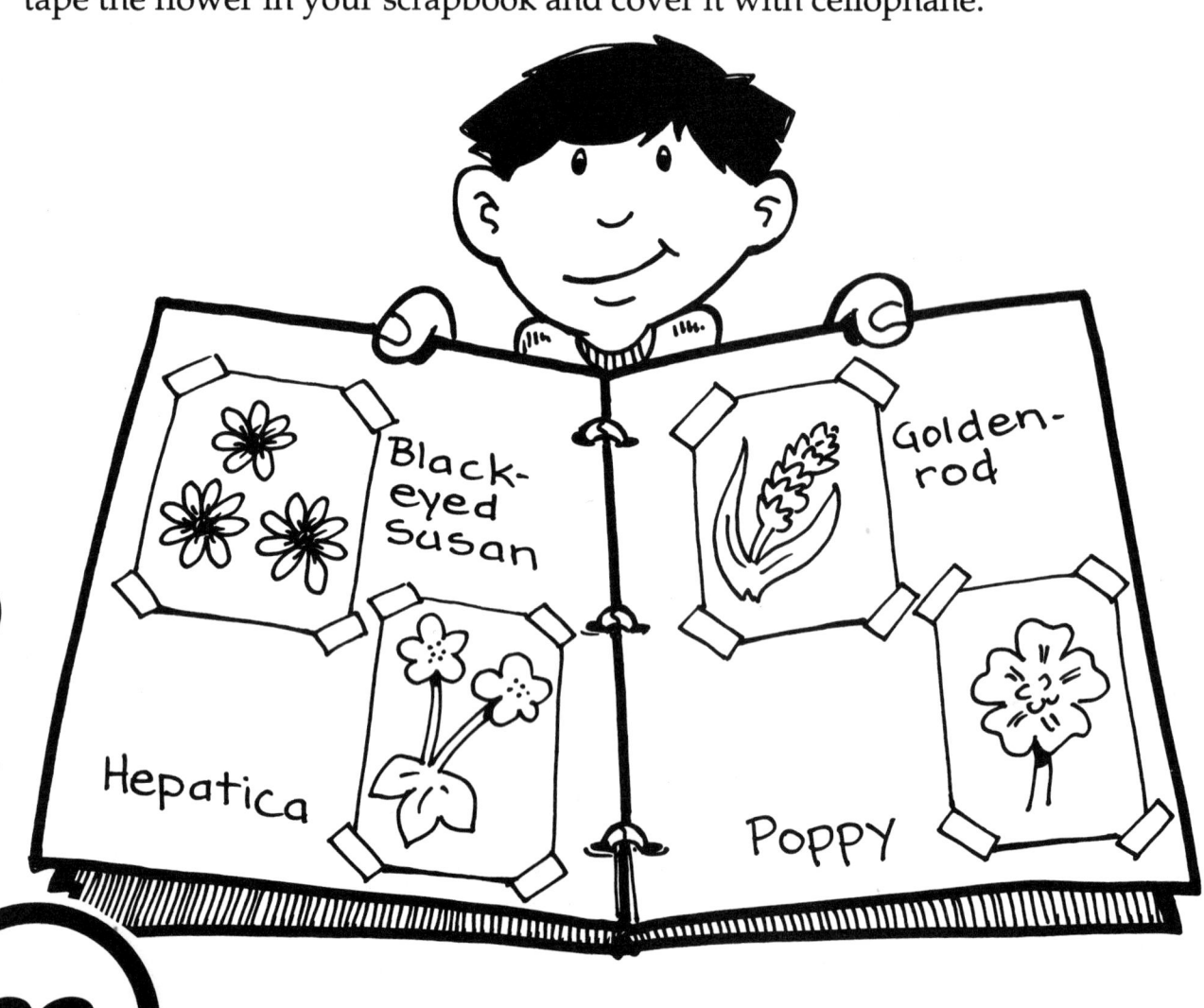

Make a Tree

Only God can make a tree, but you can shape papier-mâché to make a model of a green tree for your room.

Materials
2 bowls   Warm water   Old newspapers   Flour
Cloth   Twig, tiny branch, or stick   Green tempera paint

Tear old newspapers into tiny strips, enough to fill a large bowl. Pour warm water over the strips and let them soak over an hour. Scoop the wet paper into a piece of cloth. Hold the corners of the cloth together and wring out the water. Put the damp paper back in the bowl.

In a second bowl, mix two heaping tablespoons of flour with enough water to make paste. Mix the paste with the moist paper. Insert a small stick into a wad of papier-mâché. Place another wad at the top of the stick and shape it to form the leafy part of a tree. When dry, paint the bottom wad brown like ground. Paint the top wad green.

A Good Place for a Picnic

One day a crowd of over 5,000 people listened to Jesus talk all day. The people became very hungry. A little boy gave Jesus his lunch—just five loaves of bread and two fish. Jesus thanked God for the food, broke it apart, and used it to feed the whole big crowd. There was even food left over! God uses our small gifts in mighty ways.

Where did Jesus ask the people to sit to eat their food? Write the first letter of each picture on the line above it.

Red

Stop signs and stoplights are warnings to wait.
Cherries and strawberries fill a sweet plate.
Fire trucks rush with loud sirens blaring.
Valentine hearts send a message of caring.
Cranberries, raspberries, radishes too,
And juicy tomatoes so healthy for you—
These things are all different in size, shape, and name…
In only one way are these things quite the same.
If you guessed it's their color, you surely were right,
For they're all cheery red—a color so bright.

Ask an adult to help you read Isaiah 1:18. Can you guess which word in that verse means *red*? God loves us so much, He let His only Son shed His blood and die on the cross for us to win us forgiveness and eternal life. The color red can help us remember Jesus' wonderful gift in dying and rising again for us.

25

Red Paper Beads

Follow the directions to make a red, beaded chain. You may make it as long or short as you wish. It can be a bracelet, necklace, belt—even a bright garland for your Christmas tree.

Materials

Red construction paper
Piece of wire
Glue
String
Shellac spray in an aerosal can (An adult should spray the shellac in a well-ventilated area.)

26

Thank You, God, for Fire Fighters

Say a thank-You prayer to God for fire fighters who work to keep us safe. Then draw a line through the maze to help the fire truck find its way to the fire.

Moses and the Burning Bush

Long ago God talked to His helper Moses from a burning bush. But the fire did not hurt the bush. God told Moses He wanted him to lead His people from Egypt, where they were slaves, to a new land where they would be free. Jesus frees us from being slaves to our sin, and will one day lead us to a new home with Him in heaven.

Color the picture of the burning bush. Make most of the flames red. Color some of the flames yellow. Color some of the flames by mixing red and yellow—that will make orange.

My Red Balloon

I had a lot of fun today
With my big, red balloon.
I used it as a punchball, then
I bounced it 'round my room.
I tossed it to the ceiling and
I laughed to see it drop.
But then my laugh turned to a frown—
My red balloon went *POP!*

Red Strawberries

God created many kinds of berries for us to enjoy. Many people like sweet, red strawberries. Draw a line to match each pair of strawberries that are the same.

The Red Sea

God mentions the Red Sea many times in His Word. The Red Sea got its name from the many tiny reddish plants called algae that grow in it. God parted the Red Sea to let His children walk across on dry land as they escaped from Egypt. Then He closed the waters to drown Pharaoh's soldiers so His children could be free. Who was the man that God chose as His helper to lead His people through the Red Sea? Write the first letter of each picture on the line above it. Then ask an adult to help you read the story in Exodus 13:17–14:31.

Sugar Tulips

God created beautiful flowers for us to enjoy. Tulips are bright flowers that bloom in the spring. Follow the directions to make sugar tulips. They will last all year long.

Materials

Red food coloring Cup White sugar
Spoon Green crayon Craft glue Toothpick

Draw some tulips on white paper, or copy the tulips on this page. Color the stems and leaves with a green crayon. In a cup, mix 1 or 2 drops of red food coloring with 2 tablespoons of granulated sugar. Using a toothpick, carefully spread craft glue over the petals of the tulip. Spoon red sugar over the petals covered with glue. Allow to dry for 1 hour, then shake excess sugar into sink or onto newspaper.

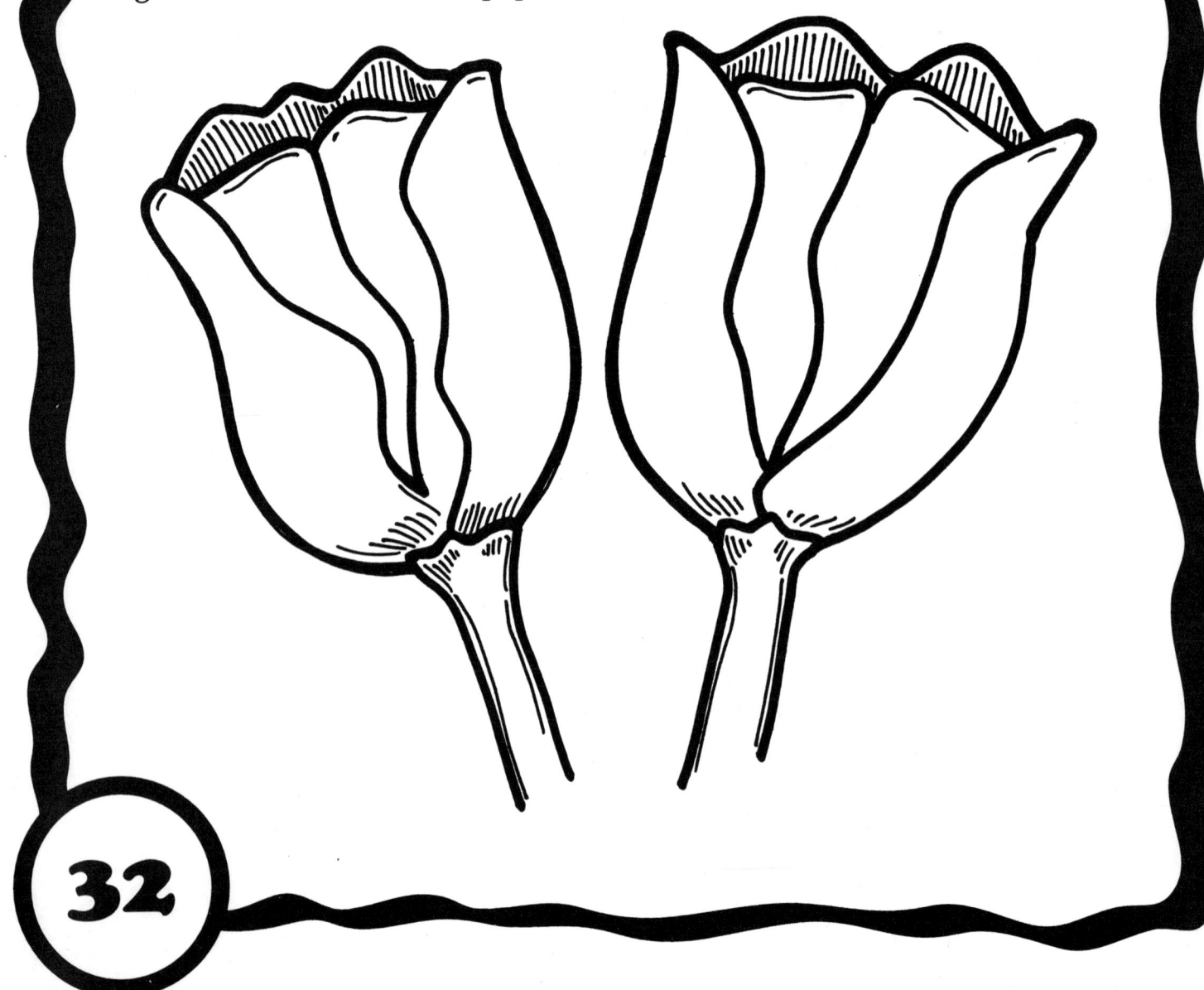